Jesus Farted and Other Uncomfortable Thoughts

A collection of essays, paragraphs and proverbs on life, people, faith and work

Jon Hurd

Jesus Farted and Other Uncomfortable Thoughts
Copyright © 2021 by Jon Hurd

All rights reserved. No part of this publication
may be reproduced, distributed, or transmitted
in any form or by any means, including
photocopying, recording, or other electronic
or mechanical methods, without the prior
written permission of the author, except
in the case of brief quotations embodied
in critical reviews and certain other non-
commercial uses permitted by copyright law.

Tellwell Talent
www.tellwell.ca

ISBN
978-0-2288-6955-9 (Paperback)

Acknowledgements

I would like to thank the following people for making this book a reality.

Nicole Fitzgerald for believing there was potential among the chaos. And pushing me to search.

Scott Lust for his generosity of friendship, and technology.

Laurie Hurd, Emma Hurd and Ellison Hurd for being such an influence of love and joy over the years.

My parents for having a middle child and for their unwavering support since then.

My Facebook family for your praise, suggestions and encouragement.

Introduction

This book may not be for everyone. You may not like it. It may not match your view of the world. It's all over the place and to call it loosely categorized would be generous. That's ok. The whole point of writing it is to promote discussion. So many people write as if they've figured it out. That bothers me. Partly because I haven't, but also because sometimes I've done what they've said and failed. I find there are rarely universal truths.

Do I have answers? Hardly any. Do I have questions? So many.

Not everything in this book will be true for you. They're just thoughts. Observations. Ideas. I like stripping down behaviors to their causes. I like calling out inconsistencies I see, especially my own. I like highlighting inconceivable kindness in an otherwise selfish world. I like making sense of things, or trying to.

Unfortunately, there's rarely new thought communicated. I just hope to present some of what has stood out to me over the years in a way you may find helpful, provocative, funny or endearing.

Thanks.

The respect of those you respect is worth more than the applause of the multitude.

-- Arnold Glasow*(1)

WORK

Working Retail in the Time of Covid

This is a series of posts I made during my 20 months working as a cashier in a large department/grocery chain. Enjoy. Or don't. Whatever. The observations are sometimes judgemental, I admit. But it's how I felt.

"The bottom line is some people are okay going to work and some people would rather die. Each of us gets to choose." Dr. Wong - Rick and Morty "Pickle Rick" Season 3, Episode 3 *(2)

I'm constantly in awe at the number of people who come through my line who start up conversations. Telling me about their day, asking about the weather and more often than not sharing personal struggles. Health, children, marriage, loneliness.

This leads me to a simple conclusion: we all want to tell our story. To share how we are feeling. To have a listening ear.

I am admittedly a captive audience but it's the part of my job I am most purposeful about. Be a listener today. Take the extra five minutes to hear the answer to "how are you doing?". And I hope someone does the same for you. As so many of you did for me yesterday.

A lady who now recognizes me feels the need to share about her life experiences. No matter how boring, involved or misguided. I now know how she feels about the Amish, big game hunting and the president.

Once the baby boomers die off, the check industry is done. 7 checks in my first 10 customers today, all over 60.

A gentleman, after I have rung up all his items, neither puts the bags of items in his cart nor pulls his cart up in the lane to free up space for the shoppers behind him. But proceeds to fully pay for his order and receive his receipt before moving.

While bagging groceries, I had the unfortunate opportunity to ask someone, "Is it ok if your banana sits on top of your nuts?"

A guy came through my line today and asked how I was. I threw a "good" his way and obligatorily asked the same. Without hesitation he said, "Phenomenal."

Day made.

Last week a lady came through my line. While I processed her order she was looking for her sister. She saw her from far away and proceeded to yell for her by name. When that didn't work she got louder. On her 6th attempt I saw her wave and shortly another woman joined us.

As she arrived the woman in my line asked her sister, "Didn't you hear me calling for you?" The sister replied, "Yes, I heard you the second time." To which lady #1 asks incredulously, "Then why didn't you turn around?!?" "Oh I was just messing with you."

What followed was one of the most soul satisfying four minutes of uncontrollable laughter I have heard in a very long time. This woman was so tickled at the exasperated look on her sister's face. I smiled for ten minutes after they left.

A few thoughts on working in retail and a grocery retail store specifically.

-No one can read a sign. (Including this guy!)

-People who speak English as a second language are 50% more likely to not understand a sale. (Not their fault but annoying nonetheless as they are also 50% more insistent they are right)

-If you shop with food stamps and your first stop upon checkout is the lottery? You don't have or deserve my respect.

-Stores should no longer accept checks.

-If you leave an item somewhere other than where you picked it up, you are lazy and inconsiderate.

-Cashiers have to keep track of like, a hundred different things. The job isn't easy and doesn't pay well.

-If you don't return your cart to the corral you are a jerk. If you leave it in a parking spot? You're human garbage.

-Sounds. The constant cacophony of noises. From beeping motorized carts, to alarms going off at the doors due to security tags to the din of items being scanned, announcements about our store performance on the loudspeakers and screaming children.

-Kids act frigging terribly in public and parents are soft for offering no discipline to curb their poor behavior. Boys are worse than girls and seem to have the market cornered on being loud and stupid.

-Management cares about what the corporate overlords tell them to care about.

-Coupons are easy to read and no one pays attention to how to use them properly. I can only assume people are malicious, dumb or ignorant.

-My least favorite part of my job is when I'm 30 seconds from finishing with a customer, another person pushes their cart into my lane. Not while I'm starting the order, not part way through, not after I've finished, but 30 seconds before I'm done. Just to rob me of the hope of having a small respite from the constant deluge of work.

-You haven't lived until you've been paid with a warm slightly damp 20 pulled from someone's bra.

-Not everybody is as enthusiastic about showering everyday as I am.

You meet all kinds of people in this job.

The customer who holds everyone hostage with his continuous monologue about how things "used to be".

The pair who come through my line only, and really dislike each other and swear and call each other names in front of their daughter.

The guy who thinks I know his first name and insists on calling me by mine.

The family who smell like they haven't bathed this month and pay in cash.

The people who insist on double bags because they have two flights of stairs.

The handsy couple who think we all want to see young love.

The people who hand you $100 for a $95 bill and ask if you need more.

The morbidly obese motorized cart couple who can't bear to shop alone, thereby freeing up a cart for someone who needs one.

While everyone (not really) in my Facebook feed works from home or not at all, here's a few gems from my week so far.

-A lady purchased a pack of toilet paper and handed it to me to give to someone who needed some but couldn't find any. Aww, nice. Go to my break, come back and it's gone off my register! Someone had grabbed it. So it got paid for twice.

-A dude went toe to toe with me over a coupon that he said entitled him to $1 off a free item. I told him that I couldn't give him money off something he didn't pay for. He asked to see my manager. I gave it to him because arguing with a crazy person is not worth $1. He probably left feeling smugly satisfied.

-A lady came through my line with two packages of toilet paper and said as she bought them, "I really don't need these but better safe than sorry right?"

-A lady came through my line and proceeded to tell me everyone was crazy and it had her going crazy and her teacher husband (which she told me three times) was home and driving her crazy and she was home with their baby (not sure it was hers or his) and she proceeded to buy $180 of stuff and complain that people who hoarded were the worst.

-98% of people have been super understanding, cordial, and thankful.

Today in work news:

TP has returned.

No reusable bags allowed.

Supposedly we are getting a weekly bonus on top of our temporary bump in pay.

Store is 50% busier today than yesterday despite the stay at home recommendation still in effect.

People look like they're going to go home and cook meth with their masks and gloves on.

The average person can't resist asking how I am, commenting on "crazy shoppers" (of which they are one) or thanking me for being at work.(which I have no choice in)

For the record, I'm really tired. More so than normal. Not looking for sympathy. No. Frig that. I am. I am looking for a there, there.

Be safe, smart and kind folks. Love, Jon

So there's this phenomenon that happens where people will walk past an open register to go to another register. No rhyme or reason. I've been tempted to ask someone why they chose to walk past 3 open lanes to come to mine.

If you were wondering where everyone in the world is today, they are shopping at my store.

In the past two weeks I've pushed in carts and stocked grocery shelves. So hard!!!! I fully embrace my choice to work a register.

I've met or spoken with at least 5 coworkers who are under the age of 23. I'm like a friggin' grandpa around here.

More men are shopping now than I've ever seen. Not sure if to be helpful or get out of the house.

Parents who placate their children with toys and candy as an alternative to discipline are doing a true disservice to their kids. And all of us really who'll have to deal with those kids as entitled adults.

Smiles make a huge difference. They really do. I'll try to get better at it.

Just because you don't have to go to work doesn't mean you shouldn't bathe. Take a shower people!!! Two if necessary.

Lots of new hires. They seem to be doing well. Nice to work for a company that's helping people stay afloat.

I constantly hear, "you guys are out of____ do you know when you're getting more? I don't need any but..."

My "bonus" or "hourly wage increase" was entirely eaten up in taxes.

Wearing jeans > wearing khakis

We are still on winter temps at work where the thermostat is controlled in Michigan (or so I've been told). So I sweat through the day in a shirt that doesn't breathe.

It's neat talking to coworkers and hearing about their lives. Many will tell you a lot that's going on furthering my inherent belief that we all just want to be known and accepted.

People need to learn how to load a grocery belt. There's now a huge piece of plexiglass on each lane for more of your stuff to run into. Please at least pretend to be aware of the chance of your bread smushing.

A woman stole our bottle of sanitizer that we leave out for customers. She was buying two but still felt the need to take ours.

Shopping is not slowing down. I dare say people are getting bolder. They somehow believe their painter's masks and gloves will protect them. Just a regular Saturday.

Nobody listens anymore. I can't tell you the number of times I say "hello", to be met with a "Great! How are you?" Or I say good night as they're leaving and they thank me and say "you too", like I'd said "have a good night". Isn't it common to just say good night back?

So much theft right now. Blown away.

I see the same people come in... Every. Single. Day. This is infuriating.

I don't wanna know how bad your life is when you have to come to the store to "get out of the house."

Getting my temperature taken every shift now.

Still like my coworkers. It's like we're a ragtag bunch of people trying to withstand the onslaught of interlopers. There's community in common experience.

Busy day at work. Wall to wall customers. Overwhelming. But made better by three people.

A young supervisor who always calls us the sweetest names.

A guy who asked how my day was and in an unguarded moment I answered "not great." He said "well it's about to get better". Ok, I said. Unbeknownst to me, he had already placed a treat on the belt for me.

A lady who told me she usually shops at night because she doesn't like people. We shared a good laugh.

They are now paying people to stand at the entrances and count the number of guests who come in. It's actually fun.

The amount of guests who get cash back so they can immediately funnel it into the lottery machines would stun you.

This store is where I experienced my first lunchable. I'm partial to the bologna and turkey.

You don't realize how many different parts there are to your feet/legs/hips until you've stood for 40 hours in a week. And they all feel bad.

It's stupefying to watch someone go through a 12 items or less self checkout with 30 items at the same time as someone with 3 items get in line behind someone with a full cart in a regular line.

Bandanas, painters masks, swiffer cloths, handmade masks, surgical masks. Seen then all now.

Update! Scarves, random pieces of cloth, T-shirts...

Sold some tiramisu Oreos yesterday.

In the bad news/good news vein: There was a bloody, used piece of cotton on the floor of my lane. There was also a loose $20 bill.

When you ask if the busyness has died down, you will receive a blank stare. No. No it hasn't. You cretin.

One of my coworkers, who knows everything about everything, was paid entirely in ones. For a $130 order.

It's Wednesday and the store is full. Wednesday.

I don't remember a time before everything smelled like window cleaner.

Spoke with a gentleman who will most likely lose his small business because of all this. It's too easy to overlook people's struggles until you hear about them.

Just know, if you wait in my line while other lines have no waiting, I'm silently seething.

This week I've been on two lanes of opposite frustration. One you couldn't use the pen on the screen. One you couldn't use your finger.

There is some magical spell that comes over folks when they have to grab their groceries off the rotating console. They grab them by the wrong handles. They grab them too fast. They take bags off when more can clearly go in them. They feel the need to double bag items that don't need it. They steal extra bags. They just stare at them when I start piling groceries up top as I run out of room to bag more.

There's a guy at work who walks so slow he's only a hair above motionless.

I learned yesterday it's impolite to ask my black coworkers about their hair. So....you're welcome, everyone else I know.

The amount of times a day I'd like to cuss someone out would probably floor you.

None of us are really working longer hours right now but the work feels harder. I'm not sure why. I know I've had to answer more questions than I normally do.

Some guy came in and bought 39 cans (or our entire supply) of unsalted green beans for his dog. Then proceeded to tell me everyone else is out of them and he can't understand why.

I've witnessed two people pay for someone who didn't have enough money to pay for their groceries and two people offer to accompany someone out to their car to unload groceries.

"Look for the helpers." - Mr. Rogers

When someone asks, "How you doin'?" and I say, "Great! How are you?", at least 50% of the time they don't answer me. At all.

Work feels like I'm back in high school. There's the cool kids, the nerds, and everyone else.

People have become way less picky with what they want in their bags. All the "bring their own bag" people want as few as possible. And everyone else just wants to get out of the store.

Masks I saw today: plastic bag, scarf, towel, bandana, T-shirts, surgical masks, painters masks, sleeve covered arm.

I've become truly enlightened by the general public as they get to the bottom of this pandemic. I now know:

a) it was predicted in the Bible

b) it was created by the Chinese

c) it's the Democrats fault

d) it's the Republicans fault

e) it's a conspiracy of worldwide proportions

f) it's almost over

g) it's going to last 2 years

h) it's going to change everything

i) it's not going to change anything

There are people who, when the payment screen doesn't respond the way they want, just tap it harder. Like that will somehow make either the pen or screen respond better. I mean, they use force to the point of possibly breaking the thing. Hate to see how they treat their phones or computers.

I have customers who will ask me if they have all their bags while I'm turned away from them. How would I know?

Some people don't like the way I bag stuff and they rearrange their bags or double them. I'd do what they want if they'd bother to instruct me.

There is no slow down. They say unemployment is at 20%. Ok. But no one is curtailing their spending. The shelves and stock will never recover if it doesn't stop flying off the shelves as fast as it gets put out.

On a serious note, a coworker received some unwanted attention in the form of a note from a much older customer. It wasn't graphic but it was very inappropriate. I feel for women in general who have to deal with men who can't behave the right way.

I was lifting something and felt a pop between my shoulder and bicep. There was pain. It's still sore but not debilitating. Massive bruising.

They turned on the air conditioning!!! Now I only have to sweat on the way to work and back home. (No AC in the car)

When people hand me crumpled or folded bills facing 8 different directions, I always take my time and straighten their bills and slowly get their change to them.

We have rules at work. Sort of. We have rules that apply if you get caught. Dress code, clear bottles for water, bathroom breaks, talking between lanes. It's all so randomly enforced that it makes my brain hurt.

I watched a man struggle with his face mask. He had put the ear elastics over his head down to his neck and couldn't figure out where to put the top one.

Based on what's being sold here during the 'Rona, I should have been a vintner.

Just watched a lady fill up her soda cup from another store.... at my store.

After 3 weeks of working 2nd shift, I no longer have a sense of what time it is. It is a strange feeling.

I know between 80 and 90 codes for fruits and vegetables at work. I'm not bragging.

We had a tornado warning about 15 minutes before I left the store the other day. I shopped a little before leaving but was accosted by someone who couldn't find something. So - off the clock - I helped him out. It delayed me enough to be caught in a deluge as I was walking out. Before I left someone was walking in. During a monsoon. And a tornado watch. Didn't want to wait it out...

There are people who shop our store for their own store. They seek out new cashiers so as to get more items then they would normally be allowed.

So in covering the greeter breaks there are a few responsibilities. You have to wipe down the carts with a cleaning solution and hand out wipes for anyone who wants one. 99% of people wipe down the cart even with the knowledge that they've been cleaned. They also take wipes for their hands even though there's a sign saying "please don't use for hands". They also take multiple wipes even though there's a sign saying "one wipe per person". I had two ladies get upset at the fact that I had handed them their wipes. Which is how it's done. They said my hands weren't clean.

Had a fella come through my line who felt the need to tell me how bad it is for me to wear a mask all day everyday. Like it's my choice.

Yesterday I was a witness to a family squabble. A grandmother and grandfather getting into it with their granddaughter and her boyfriend. Swearing, disrespect, threats of violence. It was sad to hear.

I see daily how age affects work ethic. But I also was a lot lazier in my 20s than I am now.

You're allowed to return things again at the store. Now we just need to work on getting rid of the constant over sanitizing, and masks.

Social distancing has people all over the place. There's the folks who stay 20 feet back, the ones right at 6 feet and those who invade personal space and invite complaints from every crabby person alive.

Bonus: witnessed someone wearing gloves so as not to touch anything or be contaminated. Came time to pay:

gloves came off, cash pulled out and licking of fingers to separate bills which were then handed to me.

There's a phenomenon that happens as I do my job. People will start grabbing the bags off the carousel before I've either finished packing them or while I'm still packing them. They just start turning it. This confounds me.

Would you walk into a bank, ask for some cash and grab it out of the teller's hands while they're still counting it? Why not? It's your money.

Would you walk into McDonald's and grab your bag before your food had been put in it? Why not? You paid for those fries.

Was called fascinating by a coworker. Not gonna lie, it felt pretty damn good.

A couple came through my line who I used to know from our early church days. They didn't recognize me but the gentleman commented on what a fine job I was doing. It caused the fella behind them to say how good it was to see someone take pride in their job. It's true I guess. Somewhere out there is a guy who's amazing at making French fries. Or cleans toilets better than anyone.

I can't believe there is still no hand sanitizer consistently available. At least where I want to buy it.

We can't have our breaks in the public eye anymore. Some guest thought it looked unprofessional and boom - that privilege was gone. No cafe area, no benches. Gotta sacrifice 1/3 of your break to go take your break.

A fellow cashier was amazed that so many people knew me and said hello. Going to a church of 2500 people for ten years will do that.

I earned my highest check yet last week for working Memorial Day. Times 4 I'm still not sure it would be enough to live on. I really don't know how some folks do it. Respect for those doing their best.

Worked with a fever and flu symptoms last night. More than one person told me I needed to go home. Mother in law said she'd never seen me look so sick.

On my way home, there was a train stuck on the tracks. Had to take a ten minute detour. 4 hours later my youngest daughter vomited all over her carpet.

Mopped up chunks but didn't have the mental fortitude or energy to clean it up until 12 hours later. Slept fitfully until 11:30 the next morning. Home with Ellie on my "day off".

Scheduled 2-10 tomorrow and feel like hot garbage. Adulting is hard.

This Saturday is the end of our hourly raise. Because you know, the risk is over and we're no longer going above and beyond. Genuinely grateful to have had the opportunity to make more money for just showing up.

A gentleman came through my line and was wearing his mask below his nose. Consequently he didn't notice the 2 inch trail of snot escaping his nostril and sitting on the outside of his mask.

A lady was complaining about the price of cereal and how it wasn't in the right spot. How could we not get this right? She then proceeded to put her card in backwards when paying.

A guy was second in my line. Felt the need to comment on the conversation he overheard ahead of him, tried to bait me into giving an opinion on something controversial and then make it sound like he was joking, and was fully confident in all he said.

I'm alternately a monster for not wearing a mask or an idiot for wearing one. Meanwhile more finger lickers and half mask wearers come through my line every day.

There's this annoying couple that shops every week at our store. I remember them from my first stint with the store. They're retired and have nothing better to do. The wife is uber annoying and analyzes everything you ring up. They always ask for paper. And there only can be a certain amount of weight in the bags. The husband has a face that screams, "Punch me!!!" Never smiles. They always have coupons they have to search for.

I crave consistency. Especially in my workplace. What I get is mixed messages. This is a certain way. Unless it's not. This is a rule. Unless no one catches you. This is something we don't do. Unless someone puts up enough of a stink.

Rain checks, untucked shirts, taking breaks up front, cell phone usage, acceptable drinking vessels, key dumps, leaving your lane, name badges, proper pants.

I had a guest complain that they couldn't believe we couldn't keep the shelves stocked after six months of this. (Competing store) could, so why couldn't we? I can't believe we're still open frankly.

I have people come through my lines with black lives matter shirts and love is love shirts. Five minutes later I see F$&k ANTIFA shirts and F@&k your sensitivity shirts.

I was stopped coming into the store yesterday because I'd forgotten my mask in my car. As I went out to get it I was nearly run over by someone not stopping at the stop sign and who just kept going.

I had a guest pull down her mask to speak with me because she couldn't "hear with it on".

I love it when old people shop like teenagers. Pastries, chocolate, munchies. So funny when you just don't give a damn anymore.

One of the worst things about this new era? Can't hear. Anything or anyone. Masks, plexiglass, ambient noise. It's tough. And we're not adjusting well.

Strangely, two things happen all the time. People always put their vitamins with their cleaning products. This is weird because you ingest them. And they always put their pepperoni with their cold stuff. This is weird because it's not a refrigerated product.

There's this song that's part of the store's soundtrack and one of the lyrics is, "Can you hear me? Can you hear me running?" Ummm. No. But I can smell you watching.

There's a pretty regular professional shopper who comes through my line. The woman before her was attractive but didn't say two words to me. The shopper remarked that she might be pretty but she was lacking in the personality department. I observed that in my previous time with the store I'd been regularly flirted with. Now this was 15-20 years ago. But it got me thinking and I confirmed it: I haven't been flirted with once in 8 months on the job. Just saying.

So there's apparently a coin shortage. This has caused us to make the self scan checkouts "card only". People are freaking out. "This is the first step to the government making the world cashless!" "I'll just shop somewhere else!" Sarcastically asking if I'm 'taking cash'.

I witnessed my first incident of someone not wearing a mask and being confronted. It's now a "requirement" in our city. But unless something is enforced it's really just a suggestion.

So my theory is that people are spite shopping. You won't open everything? I'm going to blow all my money on popcorn and clothes I can't try on. You won't let me do what I want? I'm going to go out everyday to the one place I can and hang out.

I've been mistaken for a manager 5-6 times.

I am consistently told by customers at work that I do the best job of bagging groceries of anyone they've ever come across. Yep. Pretty great at changing light bulbs too. And cooking spaghetti.

I had a couple come through my line a couple days ago and the woman had picked up yellow bananas and some green ones. The fella was incredulous and asked her why she got green ones? She responded that they would turn yellow. He said to her - I kid you not - "no babe those ones don't turn yellow. Some are just green." And they put them back.

No jeans allowed. I guess we looked incredibly unprofessional. Glad they nipped that in the bud.

I try to pay close attention to this: when I give people their receipt or change, half the time (!) they do not look me in the eyes. Weird. Right?

For the last time, NO!!!! Being busy does not make the time go faster!!!! Stop saying it. Please. Please. Please.

I was going to rail against small talk and how much I hate it but then I have a genuinely nice interaction with a fellow and it all goes out the window.

There's a person at work who is a real life weeble wobble.

Shared from a coworker, this lady came up to the checkout and full on lit into her for the store not having crunchy peanut butter. And blamed her for not having it. Really let her have it. Over peanut butter.

There's a lady who shops with us who has her head shaved up the back like the Amish do. But it's also shaved in the front about two inches past her hair line. Also, tragically saw a real, honest to god mullet on a guy.

Bagging 101: Giving you the dos and don'ts for proper bagging because I'm a glutton for sharing unheeded advice.

Boxes with boxes when possible. Cans six to a bag. No doubling required.

Produce together. Raw meats together.

Double bag glass items.

Cleaners by themselves.

Bread with chips.

Cold stuff together.

No bananas, eggs or bread on the bottom of any bag ever.

When in doubt: ask the customer. They will tell you.

I work with a kid who I've called the same wrong name three times now. I feel bad about that.

I had a rotten bag of potatoes come through my line the other day. The customer couldn't tell. It smelled genuinely of fish. Stuck with me for a while.

Why does every customer feel the obligation to, when witnessing me not ringing up groceries, comment that I don't look busy and they'll give me something to do? Do I go to your place of work and see you doing nothing or wasting time,(which I know happens in many jobs) and comment that you should've been doing something?

The inference that someone at rest is lazy or should be occupied at all times is unfair, ridiculous and something I would physically fight someone over.

Two guys in my line bonded over their love of a certain former president and proceeded to get misty about the future when he would undoubtedly take office again. That, and their shared affection for guns and ammo and what they plan to do with it if what they want to come to pass does not. Not exaggerating.

There is nothing but the stream of people who continue to shop and shop and shop...

A customer came through my line to buy a gift card for a certain restaurant because they were 10% off and she couldn't find one. I found one and tried to ring it up for her only to find out there was something wrong with the card and every one like it. No rain check available, no card available. This is life at my store.

People, for some reason, (because they've been damaged or something) cannot refrain from jamming their credit cards into the reader. Jam it in, rip it out. Angrily. Like it abused their children or something.

In the last two months we've lost ten people and hired maybe 3?

One of my last guests of the day bought one jug of detergent and handed me three coupons for it. Three.

There's a father and son who come through my line. I haven't seen them in a few months but the son seems like he was the product of an incestuous relationship. The man never smiles and always pays by check. One or both of them smell like an unwashed butt. And it lingers.

A lady was frustrated with me for packing her packaged lunch meat on top of her packaged pork. Even though I wrapped it in an extra bag. She said raw meat should never go with a cooked item. I told her I wrapped it and she told me that the health department would be very upset with me. I just smiled, as she had placed them on the belt directly on top of each other.

There's a guy who covers the dairy department basically by himself and works between 70 and 80 hours a week.

When we get overwhelmed with customers (which is everyday) the lead cashier calls a dept. 20 which means any available management should come and run lane. I'm tempted to scream "NO, WE GOT THIS. WE'RE FINE!" (Sarcastically) but that would be unnecessarily rude. A funny thing happens when things have calmed down though (relatively speaking). The managers always seem to have a get together. A chat. Weird.

Jesus Farted and Other Uncomfortable Thoughts

FAITH

Faith Steaks (knife and fork)

-Jesus farted. An irreverent statement to some but not intended for shock value. It is meant to comfort. The God of the universe was pushed out of a vaginal opening. He soiled himself. He skinned his knee. He scared his parents. He was hungry. He got angry. He cried. He joked with friends and drank wine, belched and yes, farted.

But the most heartening part to me is this: he was tempted. Not just to call angels for help or show off his inherent godliness. But to look lustfully at other humans. To be selfish. To lie. To steal and cheat. To hurt people. To insult and make fun of others. To run away from God. To abandon his mission.

He sees our weaknesses not with the eyes of a disappointed parent. Not with the judgement of an over expectant boss. Not with the superiority of a holier than thou group of the religious elite. No, he sees our weaknesses as one who was tempted in every way we are and feels the sympathy and empathy of one who has been there before.

One of the things I loved about Donald Sutherland's performance in "The Hunger Games" *(3) was his explanation that hope, "is the only thing stronger than fear" and to a conquered people, could be revolutionary. And therefore dangerous.

Some hope for things like financial security, ongoing health, happy children. Others hope for a new job, a cure, a way out, help to come from any source.

There's a line from an old hymn that says, "my hope is built on nothing less than Jesus' blood and righteousness". That sentiment is wonderful and true for me. It speaks of the foundation of my hope. The frame of my hope however, is built with the people in my life.

I'm hopeful because in spite of a pandemic and frustration and depression and job loss and anger and division that runs deep, I am still able to see the best of us. In small kindnesses. In words of care. In gifts. In openness and understanding. In the glacial change in my own life.

I want my hope to be dangerous. And to impact the world.

-One day while working as a cashier, I noticed a guy after he had gone through my line and was leaving. He was wearing shorts and his lower leg just above his ankle was covered in what I can only describe as a wet scab. I don't know what gangrene looks like but it was as close to that as I could imagine. He didn't seem like he was in pain, and he didn't seem to mind that it was staining his sock.

It got me thinking about the hidden infections we walk around with that may be slowly killing us. Fear, resentment, anger, trauma, addiction, greed, selfishness.

"There is a Balm in Gilead" is an old hymn that used to be sung in churches. It speaks of Jesus as the healer of our souls.

About a month later, the same guy came through in a wheelchair. His lower legs were gone.

What are the things that we cover or don't want to acknowledge? Where is your soul bruised?

I pray we may all seek and find the strength to deal with what ails us.

-I just watched a child in a full on tantrum get a ride on the mechanical pony in the grocery store. This was after being carried kicking and screaming the length of the store by her father who kept telling her to "stop it" in his indoor voice.

There's no place on earth I wouldn't have exited immediately with my child if they were throwing that kind of fit. To discipline them privately or publicly on the way.

I don't know how my kids will turn out. I don't know how that little girl will either. I just know I'll feel mostly good about the kind of decisions I've made in bringing up humans.

Please and thank you. Respect for others. Looking people in the eyes when you speak to them. Chores. Responsibility with money. When to say yes and no. Loving themselves. How they matter to God and what he did to show them.

The rest is up to them.

-One time when I was a teenager, I played poker in the room behind the stage of our church. Just an informal game, nothing on the line. I remember my mother got upset with me when I told her about my afternoon. She said playing cards didn't have a good reputation and that I shouldn't have done it. Especially in church.

This stuck with me as I've always been a pot stirrer. Someone who asks 'why' way too much. Why would it matter? To God first of all and secondly to people.

I grew up in a church culture that didn't just love God, it revered and respected God. Rightfully so some would say. They tended to show this by taking many things that had connotations of "sin" or bad behaviour and making them off limits, against the rules, or at the very least, frowned upon.

The funny thing is - as I've grown, matured, learned and experienced - many of these rules put in place were overbearing, silly or just plain wrong.

And the worst part of this, the most impactful consequence, is that many people who would otherwise have embraced the message of the gospel and God's love, now can't stand this image of a teacher with a stick standing at the ready to whack hands.

-You could say I'm a nostalgic guy. I bought a CD of Amy Grant's greatest hits (I know) and I'm listening to it and the song "Love will find a way" comes on.

As I pull into the Tim Hortons drive thru, they must think I'm going crazy because the lyrics just overwhelm me and my eyes are leaking badly.

"Love will find a way. How do you know?

Love will find a way. How can you see?

I know it's hard to see the past and still believe, love will surely find a way." *(4)

I'm so lucky to have come from a faith background that believes you never give up on people. No one has given up on me. They still pull for me and still think I can make a difference.

I am constantly in communication with folks who need this encouragement. They've been hurt, they're dealing with loss or sickness. They are struggling with worth, with job loss or financial problems. Their family situations are garbage. They have no one reliable in their lives. They have addictions and legal issues.

Please know... love will find a way. Talk to someone. Ask for help. Hold on to the promise that love always wants the best for you.

-I'm a Christian. So for the most part, I want to give credit to God for the growth/blessings that occur in my life.

Let me tell you, these days, personally it can be tough to find that growth or see the blessings.

It comes easier for some. I see posts that are nothing but positivity. I also see some that are nothing but negativity. For years I've attempted to straddle the middle ground. I've described myself not as a pessimist or an optimist but a realist.

All that to say, a couple days ago I wasn't having the best day. I was feeling sorry for myself for my work situation, disappointed in something that had happened at work and I was also experiencing physical discomfort on many levels. I actually said in my mind, "I'm better than this world, these people, they don't deserve me."

So I prayed. For help. To calm down. For anything really. Admittedly I don't do that much these days. I feel like my prayers don't work the way other people's prayers do based on certain unchanged elements in my life.

Within 10 minutes a customer had offered me a free hand sanitizer. Nice, I thought. 10 minutes later, someone gave me a generous "gift". Ummm, ok. Later, that 'something' that happened at work had been resolved. Geez.

Believe what you want. I can't prove anything to anyone. But I live like I believe in a higher power because of moments like this. I love and treat people decently and listen and give because deep down, I know it's what Jesus would do and he loves me and I want to be like him.

-From Hebrews 11. The "faith" chapter.

Hebrews 11:13 All these people were still living by faith when they died. They did not receive the things promised; they only saw them and welcomed them from a distance, admitting that they were foreigners and strangers on earth. 14 People who say such things show that they are looking for a country of their own. 15 If they had been thinking of the country they had left, they would have had opportunity to return. 16 Instead, they were longing for a better country—a heavenly one.

I was struck by two things as I read this passage for what felt like the first time. None of them received what was ultimately promised. They witnessed from a distance. I wish I saw with eternal eyes. The faith to see what will be and not what is. The faith to believe in a future I may or may not see come to fruition.

They were longing for a better country. A heavenly one. I think that's what we all long for. A better country. One we're proud of. That may mean different things to each of us but we most likely won't see society or life as it should be until we reach heaven.

-I made fried potatoes the other day. Some of the potatoes had started to seed and looked weird. A couple had dark spots and a couple had cuts in them that had gotten rot. The temptation would be to throw them away. But I pared them down, cut off the rough areas and used them for a delicious supper.

We are in a culture where we throw things away. Out of car windows, on the ground, down the disposal, in the trash. When they look old or get stained, when they don't match or look right, when we've lost use for them.

I've found that many people treat religion/god this way. They've come across parts of it they don't like, parts of it that are old, parts that don't fit. Parts that don't taste good.

I'm all for looking at things with fresh eyes. And correcting the incorrect. But let's not be hasty to simply throw out what we know to be true when we just don't like how it is presented.

Cause really, deep down, everyone loves potatoes.

-What, then, shall we say in response to these things? If God is for us, who can be against us?

Romans 8:31

"You are for me not against me...." *(5) A line from worship this morning got me thinking more deeply than I usually do.

Not by coincidence do we most feel attacked when we have a loss, are alone, feel betrayed, are in need.

Sometimes we feel we don't have a very good defender or to take it further, deep down we're not convinced that God isn't somehow behind all of our troubles.

He who is actually against us, Satan the enemy, seems to throw the hardest body blows when we are at our most vulnerable.

But it's in these moments that we have the unique opportunity to grow closer, love deeper, forgive, let go. Be patient. With the situation and yourself. But mostly with God.

Quick fixes have never been his thing. Believe me, I've screamed in anger. I've cried tears of frustration. I've lashed out with misplaced resentment. But being in the family of God I've seen so many come out the other side. Sometimes broken and changed, but stripped of selfishness and better off.

The devil doesn't dictate your steps. He may try to trip, delay, or detour but ultimately we get to choose how a situation will affect our future.

-Why are we so stingy with grace? Recently I've listened to stories from people about how the church does not seem to offer a place for believers to bleed, to doubt, to question, to heal. And we're surprised that church attendance is down.

If the church is full of broken people who still sin, who still need forgiveness, who still hurt people and are hurt by people, why do we abandon them?

Or did I forget the parts of the Bible where God only uses the best and brightest?

You know why we're constantly surprised and disappointed with Christian leaders who fall? Because we never knew of their struggles in the first place. They never felt safe to admit their humanity.

Please, be someone who allows those around you to make the slow, messy, arduous, not always straight journey to who Christ wants them to be.

-Just a few of the things happening in the lives of those in my circle:

A teenager who died after complications with a brain tumor, a woman who can't get an accurate diagnosis for her chronic pain, a family dealing with the fallout of trauma in their children, a miscarriage, a failed marriage, continuing poor health, housing issues, money problems, family turmoil, job loss, the loss of a parent, missionaries stranded, anxiety attacks, depression, general frustration and loss of hope.

These people are followers of God. They pray. They help. They give. They try to do right. They love.

There's a scene in The Matrix where the main character Neo stops a hail of gunfire just before reaching him and the bullets fall to the ground. I feel like this is how we view God sometimes. Like he is able to stop all the terrible things coming at us and rescue us. And when he doesn't we lose a little more faith.

That's fair. But what happens when the bullets get through?

The early church was known for its perseverance. For its endurance of circumstances that would make us blanch today. Why wouldn't God show up for these people? Why wouldn't he take the pain away? Why wouldn't he change the circumstances of those who love him? I simply don't know.

My unsettling conclusion is this: our faith in the face of life's struggles has the potential to bring us closer to God than any victory or success ever could. And shouts more loudly than any street preacher. It is our greatest witness.

Faith Burgers (something to chew on)

-I love the church. I love what it was created to be, what it is at its best, and what it still could and should be. They're some of my best friends and family.

I simply hold it to a high standard. As part of it, I need to keep myself to that same standard.

Am I loving others? Am I doing what God asks me to? Are people more likely to want to be around me than not? Am I showing grace and understanding as we journey together?

We will both fail along the way. Jon and the church. Sometimes spectacularly. It's what people do. I'm thankful for those who consider me a friend regardless of my belief system. I hope you feel the same.

-Christians, when asked about your beliefs, be whatever the opposite of defensive is. Generations of well meaning but wrong people have made the rules the main thing.

Love is the main thing. God doesn't need you to defend him. People need you to show his limitless, no strings attached, life changing love to them in tangible ways.

-My youngest daughter was out riding her big wheel this morning and something interesting happened. When I would get ahead of her on our walk she would get all panicky and worry that I was "leaving" her. But she had no reservations at all about getting 50 yards in front of me.

How like our walk with God. We get worried when we feel he has "left" us. When we can not feel his presence. Yet he is there ahead beckoning forward. As his word says" I will never leave or forsake you".

Or we become so confident in where we are or that we must be doing as he asks that we pay no heed to His presence in our wake, or that his direction may have changed and we are now off course. An opportunity to reorient for sure.

-"You can't tell me what to do."

Not selfishness but defiance. It's the biggest obstacle to true obedience in the world. There has emerged, in the past few decades, a trend that says, "you don't get to tell me how to live my life". I get to feel how I want. I get to say what I want. I get to live how I want. This is in direct contrast to how God wants us to live. The systematic, slow death of my own will. Hungering after righteousness. Serving all others in love.

-Sunday, for Christians, is a day devoted to worshipping God with other believers. Some people can't bring themselves to do that. Because of memories. Because of pain. Because of sin. Because of lack of evidence. Because people suck. Because God is silent. Because of rebellion.

Be patient. Be understanding. Be kind. Be loving. Be present. Be sad. Be generous.

Hope for the best.

-I believe in a God who speaks directly to people's spirits. I can't convince anyone of anything. On controversial subjects, on disagreements over the specifics of our beliefs, on whether or not to accept____, on how to deal with society's ills, past and present.

You need to let people know... nah.

But you're representing....nope.

Don't you think... nyet.

Shouldn't you say... no.

If I'm asked, sure, I can share what I think but my opinion is never worth more than someone's heart. My intention is to love. I will never regret choosing to emulate my savior's love over winning an argument.

-If today is your day to hurt, hurt. Feel it. Don't be ashamed of it. If you're angry, sad, ashamed, bitter, just allow yourself that. You won't ever feel better without processing those things. It may be quick, but I doubt it. Tell your friends. If they don't get it, be patient. They probably want to. If they don't help. Lose them. You don't need them. God can help, in fact he's best at it, but if it's God you're wrestling with, don't feel bad about that either.

Please do not give up on this. Yourself. Life. Loving others and letting others love you.

-Taking up your cross....

Burden or privilege? Both?

I drop mine a lot. Daily. On purpose sometimes. There's no shame in saying it. Every day you must choose to keep bearing the weight.

Good Christians don't shoulder their crosses better than anyone else. But they do keep their eyes on who carried it first.

-Don't be afraid to ask questions. Questions are more than an indication of doubt, though doubt is fine and understandable. Questions can be "working out your salvation". It's a troubling time that needs people who are aware of what they believe and why. And we need church/spiritual leadership that's not afraid to answer tough questions. And...not afraid to say they don't know the answers.

-One of the bad habits I have is not letting someone finish their thought. I anticipate what they're going to say and interrupt them.

It's dawned on me that this is how I treat my life. It's nowhere near the end (I think) and yet I keep trying to anticipate what's next or becoming frustrated when what I want to have happen takes more time than I think it should.

The one who suffers most is me and I should know better. Rushing things has never been God's style.

-The genuine surprise and happiness that washes over someone when you offer an unexpected kindness is worth so much to the soul.

It could cost $5 or time or a smile or a parking space or your lunch.

Be that for someone today. Someone you love or a total stranger. Be the hands/heart/feet/face of positivity. There's no better way to honor our savior.

-Be careful that your way of thinking doesn't overshadow your love for others.

Hardly anyone will share your entire belief system which means your love must extend its reach to a multitude of people with their own beliefs.

And if you don't think that's biblical, check out who Jesus spent the majority of his time with.

Faith Nuggets (little bites)

-The greatest expression of our faith is the choice to believe in a being who could change our circumstances but for our own good, doesn't as often as he does.

-Faith, it seems to me, is less these days about the evidence of things unseen and more about looking beyond the evidence of what is seen.

-Pure positivity in the face of problems seems spiritually reckless.

-When was it decided that 60% of worship songs would have a slow building crescendo 2/3 of the way through? Tragic.

-I am rarely if ever concerned about provision. It is my lack of personal purpose and connection that has been my stumbling block. I was told Jesus was the personal version of God and I've not always found that to be true.

-If God's plans are known and occur in his time then they must take our sins into account. The God of heaven knows our missteps and has adjusted accordingly. If that's how God's plans work.

-"I already know what's in your heart and I've been waiting for you to realize it and join me in the honesty rather than pretending to be reverent." God, to a friend of mine. Good words for all.

-Sacrificial love is the greatest love among humans. Christ's love in action. What am I sacrificing to love? Money, comfort, old habits, my pride, time, the way I think…

-Christian nationalism is an idol. When people say "God bless America" they most likely are saying "keep our nation exactly the way I want it." How about "God bless the world". That's a Christian worldview.

-You can desire all the healing god can give for a relationship but if the person in that relationship with you isn't committed to healing it as well it will not change. God is limited by our willingness.

-The best defense of Christianity is love. Anyone who spews hate in any form does not speak for Jesus and does not speak for me.

-The gate is narrow. It's not going to be made wider so we need to be guides from the broad road. We can't be roadblocks. We must stand in the middle of that wide road and offer detours off of it. We must point the way to the way.

-Struggle does not always result in loss. Pain most assuredly, but possibly victory as well. You may walk away from your encounters with God with a blessing and a limp.

-Why does it take incredible faith to believe in a God whose greatest hope is to be loved for who he is and not what he does, when it's ultimately how we want to be treated?

-If God is able and what you're wanting - however noble it may be - does not happen, it must mean he is unwilling, you don't deserve it, or you will have to wait.

-Am I living such a life of grace that I'm praying forgiveness for those throwing the stones causing my death? #Acts

-Not wanting to do something is not sinning. Having a willful heart doesn't make you holier. Think of Christ in the Garden. Obedience is foreign. It goes against our nature. I submit that it's easier to love than do the right thing. We are more like Christ when we obey than any other time.

-If we (Christians) can focus more on helping people heal with the goal being their health and not their conversion I'll bet we'll inadvertently see more people believe in God anyway.

-Lord, may I never again measure my accomplishments in dollars, square footage or the praise of men.

-It's not that I don't love God. It's not that I can't believe he exists. It's not that I don't trust him. It's not that I haven't seen his works. It's not that I don't believe in his work of redemption. It's not that I can't see him at work. It's not that I'm angry at him. I just don't always like the manner in which he does things. Pure and simple. And until I do, I will struggle with being subject to him.

-Prayer seems like it has such a high "failure" rate that you have to pray continuously in order to have anything happen. I guess it's good we're instructed to do just that.

-I don't think the average Christian understands how much anger/distrust there is towards "the church". We cannot begin to change that until we've heard it. All of it. We owe people that.

-I learn the absolute most about myself and God in those 5 reflective minutes after having yelled at the kids.

-Christianity is at its most effective when it is uncomfortable. It's true that God accepts us as we are but we can't follow him and be the same person we were and do the same things we did. Jesus made people leave or move or choose or give something up.

-God used a drunk. A murderer. An adulterer. A bigot. A thief. A prostitute. A religious fanatic. Your sin will not prevent him from his purpose.

Jesus Farted and Other Uncomfortable Thoughts

LIFE

Accidental Lessons

-There was a patch of trees across from my childhood home. We called it the woods. Just in front of the woods was a sidewalk and then a patch of grass separating the sidewalk from the curb.

Every summer I used to inwardly complain that no one took care of that patch of grass. It would get overgrown and I thought, what a shame it was that no one was responsible for it so no one did anything about it.

One day I awoke to the sound of a lawnmower. A local pastor who lived a few houses down was mowing that patch of grass. No one had asked him to, he just saw it and decided to do it. I was immediately humbled by what I witnessed.

We can either be commenters on life and simply report what needs to change or we can be doers and try to effect the changes we want to see.

-I have a confession. I keep a collection of all the positive things that have been said to me. I go back to it from time to time. Not for ego or pats on the back, but to remind myself that what I'm doing and who I am makes a difference.

Sometimes this world makes it hard to remember your value. It equates value with wealth and influence. Popularity and power. Followers and likes.

As I interact with more and more people and hear more and more stories, I'm struck by how we all need to feel valued. And when our worth gets warped by upbringing, sickness or death, relationships, or your own choices, the rebuild is a massive undertaking.

So if you're still reading, trust me when I tell you, you haven't missed your chance to be loved, to be whole, to find purpose and meaning, to recover.

And here's something to put in your collection: I'm proud to call you friend and I thank you for the impact you've had in my life.

-Borders closed. Movies delayed. School from home. But hey, at least you can come to my overcrowded grocery store every...damn...day.

There's a certain rhythm to life that I expected and indeed experienced for a few brief years. It's the life you see on Instagram and Facebook and one which I covet deeply.

I'm speaking of those who are 9-5 M-F. They have their weekends. Predictable. Plannable. Shareable. Pictures and smiles and experiences and friendships and food and fun. I've not had that in 17 years. But I don't begrudge anyone who does.

When your expectations don't meet reality there's a lingering dissatisfaction that can stay on you. Like a heavy coat everyone tells you to take off but you can't shed.

It helps to write these things down. It really does. Not to have a pity party. Or sound like an ungrateful SOB. But to share experiences. To ring that chime of similarity that says "you are not going through this by yourself, you are not alone in your feelings."

So I won't make people walk on eggshells around me. I will celebrate their victories, let them enjoy their well earned luxuries and dream of a time when I can rest and heal.

-There's a road on the way to my work. Like any road it has a few cracks in it. As I was driving this morning I noticed that in one of those cracks, there is grass growing.

The road gets driven hundreds, perhaps thousands of times a week. That grass is being constantly run over by heavy vehicles.

And yet, the grass survives. And not only survives but grows.

Sometimes I feel like that grass. Run over constantly by heavy things. Beat down. Flattened. But... I also see myself in its persistence. It survives and continues to grow. Someday it may even expand that crack by its very existence. It may alter its surroundings. Blade by blade.

-I'm in a T-shirt and boxers. Lounging on my bed. With a fan cooling me. Thinking about where to drive with my daughter this afternoon in a vehicle that's paid for. Contemplating ordering a pizza tonight which is an idea that I got from a friend on social media from looking at a computer held in my hand. A pizza I luckily don't have to go into debt to purchase.

I'm listening to classical music that I downloaded to this handheld wonder paid for by gift cards I received for being fairly good at a job I work.

I've been able to check in with family, friends and acquaintances today and ask how they are.

I'm not a thankful, upbeat person by nature. But I attempt to balance the rawness of one day's misery with the joy of another's serenity and rewards.

-People are feeling very free to say what's on their mind these days. Opinions on politics. Views on religion. Statements on current health crises. Human rights are being campaigned for. Flags are being planted left and right. Some have chosen sides.

I received a response to a message I sent today. It was thankful but also contained more. Positive words reinforcing positive things about me. The exchange was brief but so meaningful. I've had a number of these over the last few years. Thanks and encouragement. Advice and concern. Wisdom and praise. Caution and humor. I have to tell you they've sustained me through a lot. I'm grateful for each and every one.

Please don't ever, EVER, underestimate what your words, written or spoken can mean to another human slogging through life.

-You're amazing. Maybe you haven't been told lately. Maybe you haven't been shown lately. But you are.

That wit you show that makes others smile, laugh or giggle.

That dish you make that is a specialty, that's delicious, that everyone ooo's and aaaa's over.

That hug you give that warms head to toe and communicates love.

Those words you say that reach deep down and confirm, lift, praise, inspire, teach.

That thing you're doing that's incredibly hard, and causes you frustration and tears and self doubt, but also shows you how tough you are.

That care you show for the world around you. To see it become kinder, more caring, more just.

That family you're raising to be better, do better and create a better world than you live in.

You are amazing. Thought you should know.

-Over the years, I've heard from a number of women who have been sexually assaulted. I have friends who have scars that run deep as a result of these horrible acts inflicted upon them.

In the past few weeks, I witnessed at my store a woman shopping in a tank top with no bra, a woman with different colored underwear under white shorts, and two young women whose shorts were so high they constantly were pulling down on the backs of them to cover their bottoms. Why do I tell you this?

Because some men see this as culpability in what could happen to them. Like there would ever be a reason to justify the heinous acts perpetrated. This is false! No one invites sexual assault. No one was ever asking for it. No one should ever be made to feel guilty for the despicable acts of someone else.

Men, I'm speaking to you. We can change this. We need to be people that shut down disparaging talk of women. We need to listen to women. We need to educate ourselves on what kind of things men who hate women say. We need to defend those who come under attack for standing up to a system that doesn't protect or believe them.

Support organizations that help women. Teach the men in your lives equality and respect. Disassociate with people who spout untruths about this.

And church folks, believe me when I say, the subjugation of women has no place in the kingdom of God. If you've been party to or silent about assaults on members of your congregation, there will be a reckoning. It's time to call that garbage what it is. Evil.

-2019. The worst year of my life. Change in attitude didn't help. Change in jobs didn't help. Change in churches didn't help. Vacation didn't help. Change in behavior didn't help. God didn't help.

This doesn't mean 2020 will be better. It doesn't mean it will be worse. It also doesn't mean anything will change. Life doesn't always work that way. God doesn't always work that way. Sometimes you need to state what's happening and what's true. The bad and the good. We're not always encouraged to verbalize the crappy parts of life.

But it's incomplete to say there weren't good parts as well. I'm part of a family that takes care of people. I'm part of a church that wants to make a difference. I was able to see people I hadn't seen in 20 years or more. I was in need and provided for. I have some great friends. I was sent many messages of encouragement and also messages sharing how I'd been an encouragement. I was unexpectedly gifted things this year which speaks to the depths of my soul. (My main love language)

So I lean into 2020 expectantly. Of new experiences and challenges. Of joy and pain. Of toil and rest. Of opportunity and slammed doors. Of blossoming friendships and deafening silence.

Thanks for journeying with me through it.

-After 2019's summation I was bombarded with positive comments, prayers and encouragement. It revealed to me what an impact being transparent can make. This year I've attempted to sum up my days in digestible bites with a touch of humor and personal observation.

Facebook to me is a workplace, church and bowling hall rolled into one. I cherish the interactions it's afforded me. The new people I've been able to connect with. The deepening of some friendships. You've been (willingly or not) my audience this year as I've worked, played, parented, suffered, grown, changed, bellyached, praised, discovered and lived.

I thank you for that. For journeying with me. It's always more interesting with companions. So as I step into 2021, I hope you know I'm here for you. With a listening ear, a couple bucks if you need it and the belief that together, we can shape this world to be somewhere we all fit in and find purpose, kinship, healing and dare I say it, happiness.

-To suck or not to suck. That's the choice we get every day.

We can throw that cigarette butt out our window or we can join a crew that cleans up highways.

We can laugh along with the joke that's racist or sexist or we can come out and say that it's wrong or leave.

We can be the person who curses out everyone on their morning route or be the one who lets someone in their lane.

We can buy too many things we don't need or spend moderately and have some to give every month.

We can find something wrong with every choice made by people we disagree with or look for common ground and start there.

We can complain about what's wrong with our kid's behavior or celebrate what's amazing about them.

Start small. Do one less sucky thing today. Suck 1% less. That's a world I want to be a part of. A world with people who want to suck less.

-You may not feel like you're doing life very well right now. Discouragement is something that can grow even without watering.

If you're holding down a job or looking: you're doing great.

If your children are some combination of happy and caring: you're doing great.

If you didn't kick a dog today: you're doing great.

If you've helped someone this week: you're doing great.

If you've prayed for someone this week: you're doing great.

If you've looked to the heavens and questioned what is going on: you're doing great.

If you've overcome or not: you're doing great.

Breathe, eat, laugh, listen, speak, rest, love. You're doing better than you think.

-In the grocery store today I witnessed three children hit their parents when they didn't get their way and my argument was going to be: Really? People are inherently good? Really?

But then there was this mother with three children, one of whom was a toddler. She purchased some groceries including a treat for herself and a can of veggie puffs for her kids. When she handed the can off to the middle child, the little girl pulled a few puffs out and ate them then reached back in, grabbed one out, and handed it to the toddler.

The look of joy on that child's face as he realized what he had was beautiful. It radiated. It manufactured joy and caused me to smile and chuckle. All because of a shared puff.

I know this world threatens to overwhelm us with seething anger and frustration and sadness and depression. But keep looking for the beauty in the ashes. There are butterflies amidst the black clouds. There is harmony in between the discord.

-This was going to be a much different post. It was going to be either angry or self pitying but I can abide neither of those feelings right now.

If you have posted in the last few days about the struggles in your life, know that I see you. If you have raised your voice heavenward on this medium and wept and screamed, know that I hear you.

If you have kept something to yourself out of concern or pride or not wanting to be a burden, know that I feel you.

The greatest temptation in this life is to believe we struggle alone. You are not alone. If you are connected here, it proves you aren't. Please reach out, confess, scream, cry, ask, celebrate, live with us. With me. Thanks for being a part of this wonderful system of support.

Observations

-Changing your mind doesn't make you weak, wishy washy or easily swayed. When you are informed, educated and engaged, you will undoubtedly gain new understanding and perspective that will impact your previous notions about history, people, relationships and society.

It's a good thing.

-I have to assume that anyone who says, "Money can't make you happy." has no idea what to do with money.

Money would change my life. My health, my career, my happiness, my ability to make a difference.

People who say hard work and the right attitude will get you everywhere are simply incorrect. You need that coupled with a huge dose of opportunity and good luck/fortune/timing.

-Art. The NBA. Tuna.

If the world finds it valuable they will pay outrageous amounts for it. I will never understand what sets trends and what makes something worth a lot to someone.

I do know my worth can't come from what I do. It must come from what I am.

Son. Father. Friend. These roles must inform my worth. No one will ever pay me extravagantly to be these things. But if done well, they will leave a priceless legacy.

-Too often I make my dissatisfaction apparent. I probably owe more than a few apologies for this. For letting it seep into my day. For not letting the causes simply roll off my back. For making others experience it by airing it out.

There's no but. I wanted there to be a but. To justify how I feel. To turn it into a life lesson. Not today. To those frustrated when they see it, I share your frustration. To those who are patient with me, thanks. To those who I need to be more patient with, I will try.

-You don't always need to keep moving forward. That's lunacy. We sometimes fall flat on our faces. We sometimes need to retrace our steps, take another path, stop altogether and catch our breath.

There is no set speed. No right way or time to conquer, heal, erupt, regret, mourn, second guess, celebrate.

Some don't need advice, they need to scream. Some don't need correction, they need a pat on the back. Some don't need praise, they need upbraiding.

We must ease up on the oft repeated certainty of overcoming in the here and now and start living out the necessity of love and care for those who clearly aren't.

-Be you. This doesn't mean don't change at all. You can always improve. It will take work to change the parts that need to change. The parts you want to change.

But don't change the parts that make you you. Anyone worth knowing will appreciate your quirks, your uniqueness. Be the best you.

-I'm prone to bursts of anger. Frustration that spills out of me like rushing water. I get loud and menacing. And then? It passes. It always does. Like a flash flood. I would rather it be a stream or a calm brook. I hate staring back at the faces of two little girls who wonder what could have been so bad to make daddy so loud. The answer: nothing. I apologize a lot these days. I just want to be done with all this anger.

-I want to be remembered. Fondly. I want to have added value to people's lives. I selfishly want to have made such an impact that my absence will be deeply felt. I know this isn't altruistic but I can't help it. I want to know I made a difference. My soul yearns, aches for it. And I want to let the people who've impacted me this way know it often.

-Some days you're the waves, your beautiful danger monstrous and powerful, crashing onto shore

Some days you're the sand. Being slammed into, soaked, and reshaped.

Whichever your state, remember, at some time you will be the other.

-When one door closes… sometimes another door doesn't open. Sometimes it gets locked and you're in the dark, stuck in a room with no windows.

Sometimes there isn't another door. Sometimes you need to feel around for a sledgehammer and bust a hole in the wall. And make a new door.

-One of the hardest truths of life is that you may never get the apology you so richly deserve.

You may never hear "I'm sorry" from the person who abused your trust or your body. Or who stole something valuable from you: your worth or money. The people who continue to belittle your feelings or thoughts. The groups who exclude you for who you are or what you've done.

You may never hear it from them, so today, I will have to do.

I'm sorry you were ever made to feel less than you were. Because you're great. I know it's like fighting back the tide trying to believe that sometimes. But try anyway and find people who'll do it with you.

-I believe I am currently as happy with who I am as I've been in a very long time. Comfortable in my own skin. Don't get me wrong, I don't have the lithe, athletic body of a 22 year old me anymore. But as a whole person. The work continues but I like who I'm slowly shaping into.

Random Thoughts

-I wish I inspired the kind of affection I crave.

-Some people's only perception of you will be what you present online. For better or worse. Make sure you're mindful of that truth.

-Excuses and reasons. So closely related. Some people don't see the difference.

-We should never let the cost of our past take away from the potential value of our future.

-I must be careful that the freedom I seek isn't just a new set of shackles I don't recognize.

-You hope you are being thought of. When confirmed, it is an ember that warms for hours.

-I feel like I need a friend who can be a repository for all the lowbrow, off color, borderline criminal thoughts I have. And I, for them.

-I know social media is not an accurate representation of people's lives but almost everyone I know does more with theirs. I need to become more actively involved in making my life what I want it to be.

-It's sad when a position is taken that is not only in opposition to someone's idea but in opposition to them.

If you have to attack or tear down to have your opinion you really don't understand dialogue.

-Don't just be a source of kindness. Be a source of unexpected kindness. The impact of these small surprises of grace will shine brightly through many dark times.

-We may feel ugly and rotten at times. But we are still useful and important and can be remade into something beautiful.

-Having someone believe in you may be one of the most powerful things you can experience in life.

-Sometimes I resent when life is trying to teach me something. Sometimes I find meaning everywhere.

-Don't ever think you aren't making some kind of impact, difference or change by your daily ability to show up and keep at it.

-I hope I'm genuinely funny. Like, not funny because I say inappropriate things or things people are too polite to say. Or use the F word more than some. I hope I have a grasp of wit and sarcasm and humor that connects with people.

-Everything isn't terrible. Everything just feels terrible. Seek to pull back the veil on this world. Uncover the best of it. Highlight it for others.

-I'm always touched by kindness from the most unexpected places and disappointed with indifference from the places I most expect kindness.

-Love extravagantly. It will never cost as much as it's worth.

-The tears of failure and frustration you cry today will water the success and happiness of your future.

-Support comes in many forms. Find the one you are best at and do that.

-The verbal frustration I show when I'm inconvenienced is jarringly disproportionate to the voice I give to things that should upset me.

-Our scars tell a story. Of winding roads and skinned knees. Amazing victories and growth. Horrible failures and loss. Don't hide them. Let people hear the stories behind your scars.

-Embrace the impulse to listen. Resist the temptation to fix.

-When we remain committed to getting better we cannot help but positively influence those around us.

-Merit is just effort recognized by someone in power.

-The strong opinions I hold tend to be about unimportant things. This makes me question myself. It also makes me really like myself.

-The gentleman next to me is having a very funny conversation in another language. His giggles are hilarious. I love the universalism of joy.

-Balancing what I don't know with what I may be capable of is a delicate act indeed.

-You are what you consistently do.

-Inject all the love/positivity you can into the world right now. If you knew a tenth of what was happening in it and to it you might never stop weeping. Be a buoy of safety in an ocean of hurt.

-Some days the clouds split and bring sunshine and you bask. Some days they bring flood waters and you drown.

-Just remember, when someone posts a better way, problem solving tip, or helpful solution, they most likely have come to that conclusion after having failed at it. There's great value in other's defeats.

-Brevity in a speaker is a highly underrated quality. You may not believe me after reading this book but I appreciate the economy of words. The Gettysburg address was 272 words, God spoke the world into existence in 4. What will the impact of your words be?

-There is someone, somewhere doing something you love better than you do. That in no way means you shouldn't do it. Do the crap out of it. Be the best in your: country, state, county, city, neighborhood, home.

Trivial Information

-One of the defining trends in my life has unfortunately been my struggle to stay healthy. No, I don't have a wasting disease. No, I'm not hobbled by a challenge from birth or injury. But I have, since very early on, experienced an inordinate amount of injuries/maladies. I always got the sense that sharing any of these injuries exhausted people. I've never taken the time to fully write these down but I told myself if I ever wrote a book this would be a part of it. So this is my intentionally definitive list of physical things that have gone wrong with Jon. For no other reason than to hope that when I grunt getting up from a chair, there is less eye rolling.

-When I was little, I hit my chin on our vanity and bit through my lower lip, requiring stitches.

-At least twice that I know of, I cracked a growth plate in my foot which required a cast.

-In junior high I was hit on the thumb by a pitch and again needed stitches.

-My hip was jarred out of joint by a fall and I have two screws holding it together.

-I jammed my knuckle catching a football in gym and can't squeeze that finger without pain.

-I destroyed the ligaments in my right ankle which required an air cast for a year.

-I poured boiling water on my hand and had second degree burns which left my hand sensitive for two years.

-I was tackled playing pick up football and we both landed on my shoulder which led to 2 separations over the next two years.

-I had uncontrollable nosebleeds for a few months in college.

-I landed awkwardly on my knee during a pick up football game in college and it has been wonky ever since.

-I had to snap my dislocated finger back into place after catching a low pass in basketball.

-I lifted a not-at-all-heavy box at work and crumpled to the floor with the first of what would be a few issues with my back.

-I landed on my knee playing volleyball and I now have an ever present swelling and weakness that has never abated.

-I ran shoulder first into another player while pursuing a basketball and jammed it to the point of exacerbating the old injury which was an undiagnosed torn rotator cuff.

-I tripped over the dog and have a permanent numbness in the skin of the knee I landed on.

-I have undiagnosed sleep apnea.

-I have high blood pressure.

-I have had three separate debilitating days trying to pass a kidney stone which to my knowledge is still in there.

-I tore two biceps tendons.

-I have undiagnosed nerve damage in both hands from a lifetime of using them for repetitive tasks.

-I have swelling on my right side that I can't explain. I'm just larger on one side through my trunk.

-I have had swelling on my left heel for almost two years.

-I have had a weird pain/odd feeling on my right side under my rib cage in the back for over a year. It now stretches down into my hip and is affected when I breathe deeply or hiccup.

-How can snacks be so outrageously expensive and yet the price of movies themselves seems reasonable or in some of our local theaters is going down?

In what world do the theater owners not say to themselves, "You know, if we reduced the prices of our candy/popcorn/soda by a certain percent, a greater percent would buy them and not smuggle in cheaper snacks.

How is it not collusion, which is by the way illegal, to keep the price of their snacks so high in every theater in America? There are no outliers. They all jack up the prices.

-Why is it that French fries aren't standardized? You get a burger, it's a certain weight, there's a recipe for what goes on it. You get a drink, they fill up the cup. But fries are at the whim of whoever is scooping them. Large isn't large universally. Five Guys had the right idea. Fill a container up and then throw an extra scoop on for good measure!!!

-There's a species of seabird that nests on the coast of Greenland. They reside in cliffs upwards of a thousand feet high. When the young are ready to leave the nest they must take a leap and glide to the ocean below. The father accompanies them on this jump. Not one of them does so alone.

-One of the great things about driving through the country is the unmanned stands. As I headed up to New Brunswick through Maine, I noticed many small stands offering firewood for $4-5 a bundle. On PEI they offered new potatoes every couple miles. Just walk up, grab what you need and put the money in a box. Honor system. So charming.

-When I was growing up, there were words I wasn't supposed to say. I adhered to that fairly well. Swearing was something you did in anger, when you were out of control. I had a problem with it for a year or two in middle school. Then I hit high school and really bought into the notion of swearing being the language of the uneducated or people who couldn't think of anything more clever to say.

But after I left college and began to be immersed in popular culture and culture in general, I realized that a well placed swear word was not only hilarious but could convey the feeling of a moment in a way that softer language sometimes could not. So as I embrace middle age, I've come to the determination that there is indeed a time and place for the right combination of saltiness and tartness.

-If doing nothing were an Olympic sport, I'd be a gold medalist. Which I would not receive, because that would be doing something.

-You feel like a capable adult human until you try to hang a winter coat on a wire hanger at church.

-Saturday is the smiliest day of the week.

-The next time you're thinking "man, my kid drinks a lot of milk" remember that the blue whale calf drinks 200 liters a day.

-I have a hard time putting my faith in the scientific community when they still can't even make microwave popcorn that has all the kernels pop.

-One of the things I miss about CDs and cassettes was you could look at the album notes and see all the lyrics, or check out who played the strings on what song. Details you don't get anymore.

-No one graduates from anything but high school and college level education training. We too often celebrate common things.

-While also producing 80% of the world's maple syrup, Canada grows 28% of the world's mustard seeds.

2nd place? Nepal...

-My body has started to betray me. Though it could be argued I've been betraying my body for a while now.

-It feels strange that we willingly eat corn on the cob/popcorn having to deal with the carnage that occurs between our teeth in the aftermath.

-When I hear people say, "Do what you love!" I want to punch them in the face. Maybe I love that.

-Saw a picture of a burger with a single strip of bacon on it. Still processing...

-I have learned to be content in all things, in sunburn and bug bites, in heartburn and upset stomach, in 100 degrees and no air conditioning, in traffic jams and construction traffic.

Well... I haven't. But I need to.

-There's a species of ant that has some members of its colony filled with food, ballooning their abdomen to 20 times the normal size. The other ants feed off these ants during the lean months. And you thought your job was hard.

#beingJonHurd (Things that happen because I'm me)

So in visiting a Celebrate Recovery group just to check it out, I noticed it was "chip night". So I thought as a gesture of good will I'd bring a bag of sour cream and bacon.

As I was walking into the church, it dawned on me that they might be talking about a different chip in a RECOVERY GROUP. #beingJonHurd

So... I've spent the last 20 minutes cleaning up the spilled ice cream, cherries and shards of bowl that I broke. The ice cream was soft enough but I ran into a chunk of fudge which causes the scoop to slip and slide the container into the bowl knocking it into the jar of off the island and onto the floor. So I'm out a bowl, two scoops of ice cream and $5.00 worth of cherries.

#beingJonHurd

So I just got heckled by the umpire at a softball game for not swinging at anything close. In a church league. #beingJonHurd

50% of the time I try to get soap from a household soap dispenser, I knock it over. The other 50% its squirts somewhere other than my hand. #beingJonHurd

While I'm trying to overcome a certain destructive mindset of "this only happens to me", or an expectation of the worst, I try to explain to people that it is built upon years of experiencing things that really do nothing to dispel the notion.

Case in point: I'm at my cleaning job and a light fixture swings down out of the ceiling and hits me, in the head, 5 feet away. No other light fixtures fell the rest of the day. #beingJonHurd

Anyone know if kidney pain is usually accompanied by vomiting? Or do I just have a special case? #beingJonHurd

Every time I go to use hand lotion or sanitizer that hardened booger at the end of the dispenser sends a wayward spray to either my shirt, pants or somewhere else it wasn't intended to go. #beingJonHurd

Get in line at the drive thru. Without fail, get behind someone who has apparently never ordered from a fast food restaurant. Never heard of any of the items. Wants to order something clearly not on the menu. Needs each item described. In detail. Orders for ten people. Pays by check. #beingJonHurd

Receive gift card. Go to restaurant with family. Order more extravagantly than usual because hey, it's not my money. Calculate tip. Slide card on table top hand held interactive pay device. Realize you used your credit card. #beingJonHurd

Never fails. Walk out the door, walk into spider web. #beingJonHurd

Make a list. Obsess over not forgetting water bottles for refilling. Grab coupons. Double check list and add one more thing. Grab keys, phone and wallet. Drive to store. Forget list. #beingJonHurd

On vacation and seeing 5 o'clock in the morning at least 3 times in 10 days. #beingJonHurd

Finding that one piece of weird, unchewable something in your otherwise delicious sausage, egg and cheese breakfast sandwich. #beingJonHurd

PEOPLE

Almost Complete Thoughts

-There's a scene in the movie "Molly's Game", where near the end Molly is having an emotional breakthrough with her father and he mentions that sadly, he had to read about her being attacked and beaten up in the book she'd written. He says he's going to hire someone to find out who did it and then he's going to hire someone to kill them. She tells him not to joke about that. He says that he isn't and he doesn't care who did it and that "someone put their hands on you and they're going to suffer." *(6)

And if that's not the rawest expression of how a father feels about their daughter, I don't know what is.

-I was asked by my boss once what I wanted out of my job. I answered that I wanted to get enough done and be good enough to keep management off my back.

I don't like being hassled. I'm sure that's true of almost everyone. But I also realized that my adherence to honesty at the cost of all else is a ridiculous and naive stance.

There are times when honesty simply isn't the best policy. When sister Susan performs a wailing solo at church. When your kid asks if their drawing is the best you've ever seen. When your wife asks what you're thinking.

I need to be more judicious with the when and how I tell people the "truth". Because though we all need it, we don't need it all.

-Today I'm struggling with seeing people as the tired, huddled masses. As those who are weary and burdened. As those with stories that would make me weep.

All I want to do is belittle them for being stupid. For being thoughtless and unkind. For being selfish and senseless.

And then I remember I am them. They are me. To some degree, people have been frustrated by my words, thoughts and actions. But they've also been comforted and helped. As I have been by theirs. Friends, family, random strangers. On this planet, at this time, crawling together.

To paraphrase a great quote from a video I saw today. "You don't have to say anything, just know I'm with you."

-The body is weird. I had clipped a toenail too deeply and the edge of my toe was sore/irritated. I worry about an ingrown toenail when this happens. But the nail grew back. Straight as can be.

I have swelling on my left heel that won't go away. I don't know what I did but my body is not healing. It's not getting much worse but is definitely not getting better.

I have experienced the healing of abrasions, burns, hematoma, and lacerations. But I also have lingering sprains, tears, pulls and nerve damage.

This makes me wonder about spiritual/emotional healing. Why can we forgive some things easily but some things hurt us deeply? Why are we susceptible to different damage than other people? Why do we resist healing when it would help us so much? Why do we hurt when we ourselves are hurting? Why is pain sometimes made to feel like a shameful thing?

I have no conclusions, only observations.

Some just want their pain acknowledged. That it matters they are hurting.

Some don't want to heal. They embrace their pain like a friend. It's part of who they are.

Some have scars so deep it has reshaped them. They may heal but they are different.

Some people require so much care they exhaust the caregivers. And a whole new layer of pain is caused.

Some healing requires participation while some isolation.

Some have not yet found the source of their pain and require a diagnosis.

Some are amazing "doctors" and being around them is like a balm.

If you're hurting, don't cover it up or hide it. But don't just display it and then do nothing about it. Be open to whatever the treatment is.

-One of the things that is so difficult in conversing with people you know and care about is wanting to fix their problems. Or getting outraged on their behalf and encouraging them to take action.

Sometimes people just need someone to hear them. Someone who will nod when they make a point and join them in their frustration. Who will do anything but judge them for what they've said or done. Who will swallow their own suggestions for a time.

Be that someone. I know it can be hard.

Be a safe person to talk to.

-There are people who don't understand and people who don't want to understand. This can be extremely frustrating. But how can we change minds and actions and systems if we remove those people who disagree with us from our lives?

Your voice must speak with more conviction than those who

speak wrongly or unknowingly.

Your embrace must be tight and strongly rooted in love so as to overcome the actions of those who seek to destroy what is good and right.

Your heart must have a clear purpose to suffer the slings and arrows of the arrogant and unjust.

Your head must be about you to convey the ideas that will combat the incorrect and false contentions of the ill informed.

Your legs must be strong to outwork those seeking to undermine your efforts.

-We believe lies.

Lies about ourselves. About our lives.

Lies about others. About life. About god.

Lies that success, sex, babies, pets, money, things, friends.... will make us happy.

There are glimpses of truth. Vulnerability. Everyone is bursting at the seems to tell you their stuff. Their story. Their struggle. Look for them.

Sometimes the truth is ugly. Despicable. Hurtful. Shameful.

Can we abandon our pretenses for a little while? Can we talk about who we really are? Who we should be? Who we want to be?

Can we talk about what hurts us? What we hate? What we love? Why we believe lies about ourselves?

No one has it figured out. No one has the market cornered on happiness. Keep talking. Keep seeking. Keep reaching for truth.

-When we're vulnerable we open ourselves up. We let others know about something we've failed at. We admit we're hurting and it may be our fault. We say we need help and don't know what to do. It can be scary.

Vulnerability shows people the parts of our lives we don't take pictures of.

It's risky. It exposes us to possible judgement, unwanted advice, pity, and even the chance of being shunned.

Maybe people won't understand. Maybe they'll treat us differently. Maybe they'll think less of us.

But the rewards of vulnerability are many. Deeper relationship, closer connection, strengthened trust, healed hurts and the joy of knowing and being known.

It's ok, smart even, to be careful and wary of whom we choose to be vulnerable with but don't miss out on the incredible gifts that vulnerability can bring to bear.

-I've been given gifts in my life. Unexpectedly thoughtful and soul nourishing gifts. They've impacted me so deeply because they stand out among the everyday. These gifts let me know I'm in mind, cared for, loved.

It's a big reason I'm a gift giver. I want to impact lives. I want people to feel their specialness and value amidst a world where we can be swallowed whole.

Do something for someone today. Build, create, give, clean, buy, bake, sing, fix, read, talk to, play, listen.

The impact of your selfless act may change a life.

-Kintsugi is the Japanese art of putting broken pottery pieces back together with gold — built on the idea that in embracing flaws and imperfections, you can create an even stronger, more beautiful piece of art. This is beautiful but requires perspective.

You must see that you are worth healing and being made whole again.

You must know that you will be different. And be ok with that.

You must see those helping with the rebuild as allies and not foes.

You must know that so great an undertaking cannot be rushed.

-Yesterday, a lady in my line at the grocery store noticed an older gentleman in front of her and asked if she could pay for his groceries. He was surprised but said that yes, she could and he thanked her.

I told her that was very kind and she mentioned that she'd lost her mother in August and just felt like helping someone out.

We talked about her family a bit. She told me they had been looking over her old things that day and that's why her emotions were so at the surface.

I have 2-3 interactions like this a week. People wanting to share a little part of who they are. I consider it a sacred trust. Am I doing what I love? Hell no. Can I make an impact on people by remaining pleasant and offering a smile and listening? Yes I can.

-Anxiety. Loneliness. Anger. Loss. Stress. Depression. Fear. Doubt.

Financial trouble. Breaking bad habits. Escaping abusive relationships. Losing a loved one. Confusion about identity. Searching for purpose.

There is someone who has experienced what you have. There is someone who can help with your problems. We need to talk to each other. We need to help each other.

In a time trying harder than ever to magnify our differences, reach out and find those things that join us.

-There are so many problems in the world, it's easy to get overwhelmed. I'm finding I simply can't care about them all. And that's ok. There are capable, smart, loving, gifted humans who will take up those causes.

Don't feel guilty because you can't fix it all. Just use your platform/opportunity/money/time/enthusiasm/talents for something meaningful.

It will change someone's world and you will be better for it.

On Friendship

-I had a sit down meal with a good friend and learned about his views on a lot of things. We exchanged thoughts on many different topics which we didn't always agree on. It was great.

I asked another friend's opinion on a post I was considering and she provided insight as to how it would be viewed by others. I was thinking only of how it would make me sound.

I'm grateful for others' points of view. It's one of the reasons I love being in community with people and try so hard to foster open communication.

Thanks for being that for me. Sounding board, cheerleading troupe, caring friends and diverse group of souls.

-In the company of a friend, the passage of time is non-existent.

In the company of a friend, there are no walls to climb.

In the company of a friend, my safety is assured.

In the company of a friend, laughter is our soundtrack.

In the company of a friend, I prosper.

-My friendships are built with bricks. Not straw easily blown. Not wood easily burned. Thankful for those who've done the building with me.

-If there are people in your life that just the thought of makes you smile then you are fortunate indeed.

It is a treasure you can always return to.

-The sign of good friendship is that you are able to give and receive mocking for your ridiculous characteristics as easily as praise for your laudable ones.

-Had great conversation with a friend last night. The experience left me with this:

We need to be there for each other. In anger, hurt, sadness, doubt, disbelief. All of it. Encouragement is fine and good and necessary but sometimes sitting in the ashes is what's needed.

-I'm thankful for friends who tell me the truth. And also for those patient enough to wait as I apply it.

-A surprise visit and conversation with a friend left me:

Encouraged, to have been there for them.

Unburdened, by sharing.

Saddened, that our actions and hurts can affect us so deeply and for so long.

Satisfied, to have had different points of view and just…. talked about them.

People want to be known and loved in spite of/because of all they are.

-I had a buddy message me with a potential accommodation to a setting we would be in. Based on an earlier conversation it was something he remembered that would make the location more pleasant for me.

I was touched deeply. When your feelings are not only considered but validated you can't help but know you are being highly valued.

-I've learned more about my friends this year than in any previous year. Hard things. Messy things. I can't put my finger on why.

I do know this: people are looking for family, for teammates, for true friends. They're looking for support, for solidarity, for safety, for a shoulder to cry on.

Let's be that for each other. Let's tell our stories this year. To each other. Not for sympathy or praise. But to be understood. To be known. To heal. I'll be right here.

In the words of the Friendly Giant, "this little chair will be waiting for one of you and the rocking chair for one who likes to rock and the armchair for two more to curl up in when you come again...."

Bits and Bites

-It's often said, "Hurt people hurt people." And the opposite is true.

Healed people heal people. Give grace today. Be gentle. Pause for understanding. Smile. You may change a life.

-Women tend to love their kids more than their husbands. It's strange and I might be wrong but it feels like women have a love pie and split it. Men just make another pie.

-Hang with people who will show you their scars as they tend your wounds.

-When people ask how your day is, or has been, what do you say? What did they mean when they asked? I think if we all were more intent on sharing and listening, our relationships would be deeper, stronger, richer and more beautiful.

-You don't have to have experienced someone's pain to acknowledge it.

-I think humor is a universal language. I know that I have a far darker sense of humor than some but I'm learning that some of my friends laugh at the same things I do. It's comforting knowing you're not as weird, rough or broken as you thought.

-When we listen to people's stories we are giving them a gift. Our attention. In this world of distraction it's rare and beautiful.

-I love reading people's posts to each other, especially when they communicate praise or gratitude. Remember to tell someone today what they've meant to you and how they've impacted your life. It may be that you speak love and life to them on a day they need it most.

-Some people only share all the "awesome" things happening to them. Some people only share the giant pile of crap that is their life. I appreciate those who offer both because I myself strive for that balance.

-Any activity becomes an art when the person cares deeply about doing it well.

-I'm realizing - it's finally setting in - that my expectations of people aren't outsized or unreasonable. They simply don't care as much about the things I care about. So I either need to adjust to that, be unhappy or find new people.

-A sure sign of maturity is having and maintaining friendships with people you vehemently disagree with in life.

-When we listen to each other's stories, we gain a better understanding of who we are and how we got there.

-I'm 43 years old and saw something I'd never seen before. A lady dropped her credit card at the pay window in the drive thru and the kid at the register climbed out the window and got it for her. It was amazing to behold.

-There is a play out called "Hymn". The writer wanted to write something about love between two men that was not romantic, familial or physical.

I have been lucky enough to experience this. It should be spoken of more.

-I wonder what would happen if we received the kind of commentary on our own lives that we so openly shower on that of public figures.

-Good luck to you today. I know not everyone rises with optimism. Not everyone will be treated with kindness. Not everyone will have things go their way. Know that you are thought of fondly, cared for deeply and appreciated greatly.

-We are only truly walking alone when we refuse to believe anyone has felt the way we feel.

-The greatest evidence of love is the willful decision to share a bathroom.

-A message from my dad, 11 years ago after some random fit of bellyaching.

"But we love you because you're uniquely YOU, not because of what you can do." May I never -NEVER- take for granted how lucky I am to have a family that loves me.

-I often hear "Be kind, everyone around you is fighting a battle you know nothing about." So good. But take it one step further. Learn about their battles. Help in any way you can. Walk through it with them.

-If you want to create anger, vitriol and animosity among your peer group, please, by all means, continue to bring up your political views in a public forum.

-When we marry emotion and ideas we are inviting conflict.

-Speaking the truth in love only works when the second part is more important than the first.

Christmas

I want to write this while it's still fresh. While the memories still tickle my heart and brain. Christmas is my favorite time of year. And that's because my family made it so. They caused me to love it and now I reminisce constantly.

I love it because it means things look different. Reds, greens, whites, silvers, golds. Santa's smiling face everywhere. Evergreens weighted with shiny, festive baubles, icicles and bulbs and hovering over too many gifts like a mother hen. Darkness pierced with colorful lights.

Things sound different. From the 24 hour Christmas rotation on the radio. To strangers saying Merry Christmas or happy holidays. To the crunch of your feet on snow.

Things smell different. From roasting meat and stuffing, to baking sweetbreads and cookies. Wood burning in fireplaces. Cinnamon, pine, citrus, cranberry and peppermint.

Things taste different. Eggnog, plum pudding with hard sauce, every kind of pie, homemade ice cream and way too much turkey.

Things feel different. Giving because it puts a smile on someone's face. Hugging a little longer with friends and family. Festive parties you never want to end. Imagining the scene of God born a man.

My memories are thick with all the traditions and activities that took place in my youth.

As a child, one of our church groups used to have a sleigh ride. The guys and I would take turns pushing each other off the back and you'd have to run to catch up. I remember the sound and smell of the horses. We'd always sing jingle bells and there would be hot chocolate after.

During Saturdays or on snow days we'd push ourselves to exhaustion tunneling in the snow banks or building snow forts and having snowball fights at the end of our driveway. My face was raw with cold and from being smashed with ice particles.

When Christmas vacation started we would gather at our elementary school one morning and organize boxes of food to be given to families in need so they could enjoy a holiday meal. I remember not always having a great attitude about it but I'm eternally grateful for what it taught me about giving to those with less.

My mom would have us up as early as possible to help knock out 5-6 baked goods to be served all though the Christmas break. A love of baking was nurtured.

My Nan had a bank she would fill during the year and give to us kids to spend on Christmas presents for the family. Her generosity impacted me greatly.

My aunt Carol would always bring Diet Coke for me to drink on Christmas Eve because our family never bought it. And she would always have a butterscotch pie that no one else could make. My aunt Diane didn't have children but would get up early on Christmas morning and come watch us unwrap all our gifts. There was a selflessness and love to their actions that made me feel so cared for.

I participated every year to varying degrees in a production called the "Living Christmas Tree" at my church. Everything from behind the scenes to orchestra to singing as a child. The experiences were vast and varied as were the opportunities to try new things. The light show was something to behold. As was the impact of a group effort on a community.

We used to -without fail- go to Swiss Chalet and get the festive special. There isn't a finer meal to be had on planet earth.

My mother was an excellent wrapper of gifts. I always marveled at the smooth paper and sharp corners. The bows that accompanied each one were always color coordinated.

On Christmas morning, earlier than any human should be up, I would open my door and find leaning against it, the biggest, fullest, most labored over stocking ever conceived by humans. It took an hour to unpack and provided ten times that in enjoyment. Mom and Dad would put so much time and effort into our happiness.

My Grandma always had oranges on her tree and little boxes with chocolates. There were nuts put out that you actually had to crack. She had goblets for our drinks that always made me feel fancy.

There would be at least 6 different desserts for us and choosing was harder than picking the one present to open on Christmas Eve. Rolls from McBuns Bakery, throwing cans of Sprite out on the snowy deck to get cold, the Candlelight Carol Sing at Moncton Wesleyan Church, seeing my aunts and grandmothers struggle up our slippery walk, Anne Murray's "Christmas Wishes" playing on our record player. The holiday punch bowl, Christmas crackers being pulled and paper crowns being worn, the epic Christmas night stomach ache, my dog falling asleep buried in torn wrapping paper and more warmth, love and generosity than any one really deserves.

I have all these treasured memories because of family. The kind who gives even when they can't afford to. The kind who rides you about everything but hugs you fiercely. The kind who gives encouragement when none is deserved.

I gained a second family years ago, and while I have never spent a Christmas with them, I know they are from the same hearty, loving stock. Friends, hold your loved ones tight this Christmas, never take them for granted. This year will be the first one I don't spend with my girls.

I hold all this secure in my soul. To unpack whenever an emotional hug is needed.

I know not all of you experience joy around the holidays. But I wish it for you nonetheless. To feel, smell, hear and taste all that this amazing season brings.

There's a spot at my parent's table for sure. And because of what they provided for me to experience, there's one at mine.

Appendix:

1. Arnold Glasow

2. Rick and Morty episode 3, season 3, "Pickle Rick", Cartoon Network 2017

3. The Hunger Games, Lionsgate Films 2012

4. Amy Grant - Greatest Hits EMI CMG 2007

5. Who You Say I Am - There Is More Hillsong Worship 2018

6. Molly's Game STXfilms 2017

About the Writer

Jon Hurd lives in Moncton, NB Canada. He likes movies, butter and helping people.